MW01274631

*Thanks to Janet Jenvey and also to the staff of the
London Library for their help with research – A.D.*

Text copyright © Andrew Donkin 1997
Illustrations copyright © Gillian Hunt 1997

First published in Great Britain in 1997
by Macdonald Young Books
an imprint of Wayland Publishers Ltd
61 Western Road
Hove
East Sussex
BN3 1JD

Find Macdonald Young Books on the internet at http://www.wayland.co.uk

The right of Andrew Donkin to be identified as the author of this Work
and the right of Gillian Hunt to be identified as the illustrator of this Work
has been asserted by them in accordance with the Copyright, Designs and
Patents Act 1988.

Designed by Triggerfish, 11 Jew Street, Brighton, BN1 1UT
Printed and bound in Belgium by Proost International Book Production

British Library Cataloguing in Publication Data available

ISBN 0 7500 2304 X

SUPER SCIENTISTS

THE COSMIC PROFESSOR

ANDREW DONKIN

Illustrated by Gillian Hunt

MACDONALD YOUNG BOOKS

The bright boys, they all study maths,
And Albert Einstein points the paths,
Although he seldom takes the air,
We wish to God he'd cut his hair.

Princeton University students

The janitor

Princeton, USA – 1949

I would probably never have met Albert
Einstein at all if Spider hadn't tried so hard
to spoil our baseball game.

We were all playing in the street using my
brand new ball. Spider was jealous and I
knew he'd try and ruin things if he could.

I didn't have to wait long. The first chance he got, he gave the ball a massive hit, deliberately sending it spinning over the houses opposite.

The other kids turned and ran. We were always getting into trouble for breaking windows wherever we played.

The ball sailed clean over the houses. Spider gave me an evil look as I set off to find it.

First, I had to climb over the fence at the back of the houses. I jumped up to get a grip and just about made it over. The ball wasn't there, though, and I had to sneak through a hole in the fence to next door.

I looked through the window at the back
of the house. Inside, the walls of the rooms
were covered with books. Nothing but
books.

I started kicking away leaves, looking for
my ball. I must have made more noise
than I meant to because the
next thing I knew,
the back door
creaked open.

"Can I help?" called a voice.

An old man with untidy white
hair came slowly down
the porch steps.

He wore a loose grey sweater that was all
pulled out of shape and a pair of baggy
trousers. He looked like a janitor or maybe
the gardener.

9

"What is it that you've lost?" he said walking towards me.

I should probably have run for it, but I told him about Spider and the ball.

"What was its trajectory?" he asked.

"What?"

"Where did it come from?" he said patiently.

I pointed to where we'd been playing.
He held out his hand along the same angle.
"I've looked and it's not here," I said.
"It must have landed someplace else."
The old man reached up, grabbed the
lowest branch of the tree and shook it.
The ball fell down and landed by his feet.

"There," smiled
the old man. "Not many
people get to rescue a baseball
from Professor Einstein's back yard."

So this was Albert Einstein's house.
Even I had heard of him. He was a big time
scientist.

12

"Do you work for him?"

"We work on the same things," said the old man, showing me through the house towards the front door. "Do you know much about Professor Einstein's work?" He talked to me like I was a person rather than just a kid.

"He discovered the universe or something, didn't he?" I said. The old man frowned.

There was a small pile of books on a table in the hall. I saw Einstein's name on the top one and picked it up.

"Here, he does stuff no one can understand – like this." I started to flick through the book. It was all mathematics and pages of really long words.

Then, at the front of the book, I found a picture. It was a photo of the old man. Underneath the picture were printed the words 'Albert Einstein'.

He gave a sheepish smile and showed me out.

Outside, I threw the ball high into the air and caught it with a satisfying thud.

Einstein. I had met Einstein.

The smartest man in the world

The first thing I did afterwards was get a book out of the library. It was called *Einstein and Relativity*.

It said Einstein had been born in Germany and was Jewish. When the Nazis (Adolf Hitler and that lot) took over in the thirties he had to flee to another country. He chose America.

Einstein didn't invent things or build machines, he came up with ideas. Pure ideas about the way that the universe worked.

His theories were all about space, time, and the speed of light. Einstein was now the most famous scientist in the entire world.

Dad told me a story about how a man was driving through Princeton when he saw Einstein walking down the street. The man was so surprised that he drove his car into a tree!

I had a Show and Tell
coming up next month. (Show and
Tell is this terrible thing where you have
to stand in front of the class and talk for ten
minutes. I really hate them.) I had to pick a
science subject and Einstein was perfect.

19

I read
the book, but
I didn't understand that much.
I was desperate to talk to him again. I was
even thinking of organizing another baseball
game, just so old Spider could whack the
ball into his back yard again. But I needn't
have worried.

About a week later, I was on my way home from school and I saw Einstein standing on a street corner. He looked a little lost.

"Ah, the baseball boy," said Einstein, smiling as he saw me coming.

Einstein leaned down and whispered into my ear. "I've been walking and thinking about my work and... well, I seem to have forgotten where my house is."

He was a bit embarrassed. I'd heard that he was always doing things like this when he was wrapped up in his science.

"No sweat, I can get you home."

As we walked across town, Einstein saw me looking down at his feet. He was wearing house slippers and had no socks on.

"I have to devote my time to physics so I need to reduce everything else to a minimum. That is why I do not waste time at barbers' shops," he said brushing back his long white hair.

On Main Street we came to the 'Baltimore', everyone's favourite ice-cream parlour.

"When I arrived in America, the very first thing I did was to go in here and have an ice-cream cone," said Einstein. "Come on, I'll buy you one for showing me home."

He ordered two cones all right, but he didn't have any money. Not a dime. His pockets were stuffed with calculations and formulas, but no money.

This was my chance.

"I'll tell you what," I said. "You explain to me how the universe works, and *I'll* buy the ice-cream!"

The smartest man in the world took a big lick of his strawberry cone and grinned.

"Done," he said.

Einstein's cosmos

Einstein loved sailing. He was good at it too. Next day, we went out to Carnegie Lake where he kept his boat.

"I like sailing because I am lazy," he said as we climbed onboard, "and this is the sport that demands the least energy."

We set off towards the centre of the lake.

"Relativity is easy," he said, jumping straight into the subject.

Einstein didn't waste time. He tried never to waste time.

"When you sit with a pretty girl for two hours, it seems like only a minute. Yes? But when you are having your teeth drilled in a dentist's chair, a minute can seem like two hours. That's Relativity. Everything is relative."

I knew exactly what he meant, but it couldn't be that easy. (It wasn't.)

As we headed across the lake, Einstein explained that before relativity, everyone had thought that the universe worked according to the laws of Isaac Newton.

Isaac Newton was a scientist who lived in England about three hundred years ago. Newton saw the universe as a giant clockwork machine. You could measure any length, speed, or weight and get an exact answer that would not vary or change.

Everyone believed that, until Einstein came along and showed that the cosmos was actually a much stranger place.

Einstein realized that the length and mass of an object depends on how fast it is travelling. The faster the object goes, the more it weighs and the shorter it seems to become.

This is true for all things – racing cars, rockets, planets and whole galaxies. And at very *very* high speeds, even the passing of time itself can seem altered.

The only thing in the universe that never changes is the speed of light. It is always 300,000 km per second.

Relativity is a difficult idea because it means that how the universe looks depends on where you are looking at it from. Everything is relative to everything else.

That was a lot to think about already.

"Hey! Watch out!" a voice shouted.

I looked round and saw that a much bigger boat was on a collision course with us. Its engine buzzed loudly like a wasp ready to sting.

Einstein adjusted the sail and gave a friendly wave as we narrowly missed hitting them. He turned our boat gently towards the far shore then returned to science as if nothing had happened.

"Most of my relativity was based on thought experiments and a little common sense," said Einstein. "But relativity is true for everything, from tiny atoms to massive stars and black holes in space."

"Cool," I said, brainlessly.

I already knew that Einstein had written the most famous equation in the history of science: '$E=mc^2$'.

From this formula, people realised that under the right conditions, a small amount of matter could be turned into a huge amount of energy.

Other scientists worked on the idea and developed it further. It led to the atomic bombs which ended the Second World War with Japan.

"You must have been pretty proud of that," I said.

Einstein looked really sad.

"If I had known how my work would be used, I would have become a watchmaker instead of a scientist," he said, slowly shaking his head.

I didn't know what to say.

"That's enough for today," he announced suddenly, turning the boat around to head for home. "I'm tired."

"Of sailing?"

"Of thinking. I *never* get tired of sailing."

Our boat cut smoothly through the water and headed for the waiting shore.

Trying not to puke

When I woke up on the morning of the
Show and Tell I felt like throwing up. I hate
speaking in front of people.

I got to school and found out that I was
the last speaker before the lunch break.
Great. I had all morning to shuffle my notes
and think about being sick.

The talk just before mine was Spider's. He sent everyone to sleep, droning on about the local bird life like they were his best friends or something.

Then, while Spider was still talking, there was a quiet knock on the classroom door.

It creaked open and I saw Einstein's face appear in the gap. Our teacher, Mrs Clark, nearly had a heart attack right on the spot. Einstein slipped inside our classroom and sneaked into an empty desk on the third row.

He looked over his shoulder and gave me a big, clumsy thumbs up sign. He had made a real effort to look smart. He had even put socks on – one was red and the other was brown.

I've got to admit that having him there made me forget all about being nervous.

When it was my turn, I told them everything I knew about Einstein. It just came out like I'd always known it.

At the end, I explained how some other scientists had gone to Africa and Brazil in 1919 to study an eclipse of the sun.

Einstein had predicted that starlight would be seen to bend around the sun. It did and his theories were proven to be correct. It was after this that he became famous all over the globe.

Einstein sat there nodding every now and then and when I'd finished they all clapped. It was brilliant. Afterwards, Einstein shook hands with everyone – even Spider. He was a big hit.

He stayed around long enough to make sure I got an 'A' then we sloped off outside.

I had done it. It was the best feeling in the world.

New York City - today

That summer was the best time. I saw him on and off right until the end, a few years later.

Einstein died in 1955. I first heard about it on the radio and I was really sad. Dad bought all the newspapers the next day so I could keep the clippings about him. There were loads.

That was all a long time ago. But Einstein's theories and ideas changed the way we think about the universe for ever.

His was some of the most important and brilliant work ever done in science.

The name Albert Einstein is forever linked with the idea of genius: a man who can see further and clearer than those around him.

I know how smart he was, but when I think of Einstein, I don't think of the science and the formulas. I see him in his boat – adjusting a sail, or gently correcting the rudder. Always looking ahead for the next gust of wind that will send him speeding across the water.

Timeline

Albert Einstein was born on 14 March 1879 in Ulm, on the River Danube in Germany.

1895   Expelled from school, aged 16.

1901   Begins work at the Federal Patent Office, while using his spare time to develop his work on Relativity.

1903   Marries Mileva Maric.

1905   Becomes a professor at the University of Zurich.

1905   Publishes his Special Theory of Relativity and three other scientific papers that change our understanding of the world for ever.

1915   Presents his General Theory of Relativity to the Prussian Academy of Sciences in Berlin.

1916   Einstein's General Theory of Relativity is published.

1919 Expeditions to Africa and Brazil observe an eclipse of the sun and prove that Einstein's theories are correct.

1920 Becomes famous across the entire globe.

1922 Wins the Nobel Prize for Physics.

1933 Flees Nazi Germany. Moves to Princeton in the USA and continues his scientific research.

1939 Writes to the American President to warn him that the Nazis are developing the atomic bomb

Albert Einstein died on 18 April 1955 in Princetown, USA. He was 76 years old.

Glossary

atomic bomb   a violent weapon which explodes with
great power and can destroy life and
buildings for huge areas around it

black hole   an area in space which sucks matter and
light down into it – nothing can escape
from a black hole

cosmos   the universe

eclipse   an eclipse of the sun is when the moon
passes in front of it, blocking the sunlight

energy   when something is able to do work

equation $e=mc^2$ is an equation. Each letter has a
meaning, for example e is energy, m is
mass and c is the speed of light.
Equations can be used to work
out the answers to difficult sums.

formula   a fact shown by numbers or letters

galaxy   a huge group of many, many stars

physics   the type of science that studies energy
and movement

mass   how much matter something contains

matter   everything in the world is made of matter
– it is something which you can measure

relativity   when something is compared with
something else

theory   an idea

trajectory   when something, such as a ball, is thrown,
it can curve upwards and then downwards
– this curved path is its trajectory

universe   the planets the sun, stars and everything

If you have enjoyed this Storybook, why not try these other titles in the Super Scientists series:

The Mysterious Element by Pam Robson

Marie Curie was a very unusual scientist – a woman! Determined to prove that she is as good as a man, she earns two university degrees, before embarking on her most exciting adventure – the search for radium.

Heavens Above by Kenneth Ireland

Galileo Galilei has had a brilliant idea for a telescope – the only problem is, someone else thought of it first! And as for his ideas about the Earth travelling around the Sun…The Pope is not amused.

The Bright Idea by Ann Moore

Thomas Edison is *always* busy in his laboratory. His daughter Marion decides to find out exactly what he's doing in there and witnesses one of Edison's greatest achievements – the light bulb!

The Explosive Discovery by Roy Apps

When *Alfred Nobel* moves to San Remo, the villagers are curious. Who is he? Where is he from? And what causes the explosions in his laboratory? His maid Maria is determined to find out…

The Colour of Light by Meredith Hooper

What is light and what colour is it? *Isaac Newton* isn't sure, but he wants to find out. So he buys a prism, holds it up to a beam of light and a wonderful rainbow shimmers before his eyes… What *can* this mean?

Storybooks are available from your local bookshop or can be ordered direct from the publishers. For more information about Storybooks, write to: *The Sales Department, Macdonald Young Books, 61 Western Road, Hove, East Sussex, BN3 1JD.*

47